BARRY SCRAPYARD

Keith W. Platt

AMBERLEY

First published 2017

Amberley Publishing
The Hill, Stroud
Gloucestershire, GL5 4EP

www.amberley-books.com

Copyright © Keith W. Platt, 2017

The right of Keith W. Platt to be identified as
the Author of this work has been asserted in
accordance with the Copyrights, Designs and
Patents Act 1988.

ISBN 978 1 4456 7076 8 (print)
ISBN 978 1 4456 7077 5 (ebook)

British Library Cataloguing in Publication Data.
A catalogue record for this book is available from
the British Library.

Origination by Amberley Publishing.
Printed in the UK.

Introduction

The remarkable turn of events that was Barry Scrapyard is something that is inextricably linked to the heritage railway movement in Great Britain. It is clear in this 'chicken and egg' scenario which came first, as without the locomotives available at Barry there would have been little in the way of motive power other than industrial tank locomotives or foreign imports for the preservationists to use.

The story of why Dia Woodham chose to cut up the seemingly endless supply of redundant goods wagons rather than the more difficult to deal with steam locomotives has been well-documented by many commentators. It was that decision that allowed the time and space for the preservation groups to realise the unique resource that was still available and to organise themselves into fundraising.

It is interesting to note that the first locomotive saved from the yard, LMS 0-6-0 4F No. 43924, was actually removed in September 1968, within a month of British Rail abandoning steam totally and before a lot of locos made their final journey to the scrapyard. At that time many of the engines in Barry were virtually complete and so the immense effort of restoring them to working order was a much more achievable task.

As the years went by, more and more locomotives were bought and removed to be restored at different sites throughout the country. In some cases, the locos that were left in the yard lost their tenders, as these were sold to steel works for use as ingot carriers. Many more locos lost valuable parts taken for use on other restoration projects and by trophy hunters, either with consent or otherwise.

In 1979, at a time when the impetus appeared to have slowed in the preservation movement, the Barry Steam Locomotive Action Group appeared. This was spearheaded by Francis Blake and its aim was to try to ensure the survival of all the remaining locomotives. Surveys were undertaken on the locomotives and liaisons were established between potential buyers and Woodham's, as well as financial assistance being received and work on the locos undertaken to make them look presentable.

In the summer of 1980 Woodham's scrapped two of the locomotives and this was a reminder to preservation groups that the precious resource of steam was likely to soon disappear. More supplies of redundant wagons relieved the imminent threat and eventually all of the remaining locomotives found a place within the heritage railway world, even if only as a source of spare parts.

It can be seen that the 217 steam locomotives removed from Barry Scrapyard have become the backbone of the heritage railway preservation movement in this country. Without them this movement would not have been able to expand into the successful tourist industry that it has become today.

3 August 1973, LMS Ivatt 2MT 2-6-2T No. 41312

In August 1973, No. 41312 stands on the sidings that were associated with locomotives about to leave Woodham's scrapyard, having been purchased for preservation. It would linger for another year before being delivered by rail to the Caerphilly Railway Society site, the former locomotive works.

3 August 1973, LMS Crab 2-6-0 No. 42765

No. 42765 was one of the last locomotives in the class to remain in active BR service. In the summer of 1973 it was in the process of receiving a coat of protective paintwork. It would be another five years before it moved to the Keighley & Worth Valley Railway. Restoration was completed on the East Lancashire Railway, where the engine has become a regular performer.

3 August 1973, LSWR Urie S15 4-6-0 No. 30506

No. 30506 awaits removal to the Mid-Hants Railway for renovation into working order. It would be another two and a half years before this loco eventually left the yard. Restoration to working order was very long and complex and included replacing the boiler with one from another Barry resident, S15 No. 30825. First steaming in preservation came in 1987.

3 August 1973, LMS Jinty 0-6-0T No. 47298

No. 47298 left Barry in 1974 and was restored to working order at Steamport, Southport, in 1979. In 1983 it became a resident performer at the Llangollen Railway and in 2012 was bought by Ian Riley and moved to the East Lancashire Railway.

3 August 1973, SR Maunsell Q 0-6-0 No. 30541

No. 30541 was the only survivor of this class. It was preserved and moved from Barry to the Dowty Railway Preservation Society base at Ashchurch in 1974. Another move in 1978 saw the loco arrive at the Bluebell Railway and it returned to working order in 1983.

3 August 1973, SR Maunsell U 2-6-0 No. 31638

No. 31638 had to wait another seven years after this photograph was taken before it was moved to the Bluebell Railway in 1980 and another twenty-six years before being wonderfully restored to working order.

3 August 1973, GWR 0-6-0PT No. 3738

No. 3738 left Barry by rail in the company of two other residents in April 1974. It was returned to working order by the Great Western Society at Didcot a mere two years later – quite an achievement.

3 August 1973, GWR 0-6-0PT No. 9681

No. 9681 had caught the attention of a famous name in locomotive preservation – Tom Tighe. However, the loco was rescued in 1975 and transported to Norchard on the Dean Forest Railway, where in September 1984 it moved under its own steam for the first time.

3 August 1973, GWR 2-8-0 No. 3862

No. 3862 was bought by the LNWR Society in 1987 and removed from Barry in 1989. It was sold to a member of the Northampton & Lamport Railway in 1994 and is now under restoration at Pitsford.

3 August 1973, BR Standard 2MT 2-6-0 No. 78059

No. 78059 had been a late 1967 arrival in Barry. It would be ten years before this loco left Barry for the Bluebell Railway and since then a small dedicated group has been busy recreating a BR 2-6-2T 2MT, No. 84030, from its remains.

3 August 1973, BR Standard 8P 4-6-2 No. 71000

No. 71000 *Duke of Gloucester* looks in fine fettle from this photograph. It was rescued in 1974 and it was to take twelve years of painstaking effort before the loco was restored to working order at the Great Central Railway. No. 71000 worked regularly on the national network and many heritage railways until being sidelined for a major overhaul at the Tyseley Locomotive Works.

3 August 1973, GWR 2-8-0 No. 2857

No. 2857 was rescued by a group based on the Severn Valley Railway in 1975 and restored to full working order four years later. It has become a regular performer on the Severn Valley and even ventured out onto the national network with a demonstration freight train.

3 August 1973, GWR 2-6-2T No. 5199

No. 5199 is at the head of a line of GWR locomotives. In 1985 it was rescued and taken to the Gloucester & Warwickshire Railway. In 1988 restoration to working order gathered pace and the first steaming took place at the Llangollen Railway in 2003.

3 August 1973, GWR 2-6-2T No. 5199

No. 5199 was complete with its cycling lion still looking good seventeen years on. Thirty years after this photograph was taken, the loco would be steamed again.

3 August 1973, GWR 2-8-2T No. 7200

No. 7200 was removed to the Buckinghamshire Railway Centre in 1981. Fifteen years later, restoration to working order began by the 7200 Trust.

3 August 1973, S&D 7F 2-8-0 No. 53809

No. 53809 left Barry in late 1975 for restoration at the closed station of Kirk Smeaton on the Hull & Barnsley Railway. After further renovation at the Midland Railway Centre, Butterley, the loco was returned to steam in 1980. It has worked regularly on the national network, the North Yorkshire Moors Railway and more recently the West Somerset Railway.

3 August 1973, SR Maunsell N 2-6-0 No. 31874

No. 31874 was the only one in the class to make it to Barry. I think the person working on the loco is John Bunch, who was responsible for saving a number of locos from Barry. No. 31874 left Barry in 1974 and was restored to working order at the Mid-Hants Railway three years later.

3 August 1973, SR Maunsell S15 No. 30828

No. 30828 was returned to working order at Eastleigh Works in 1994. Since then it has worked on the national network and several preserved railways, including the Swanage Railway. It is now based on the Mid-Hants Railway and is undergoing a major overhaul.

3 August 1973

A general view of the top yard at Barry showing mainly ex-GWR locomotives and goods wagons stored, ready for scrapping.

27 September 1970, LMS Stanier 2-6-0 No. 42968

No. 42968 was the sole survivor of a class of forty locomotives. It left the yard at the end of 1973, being towed by rail to the Severn Valley Railway. In 1981 its turn for restoration arrived and it was steamed for the first time in preservation in 1991.

15 March 1970, LMS 8F 2-8-0 No. 48431

No. 48431 was the nineteenth locomotive to be removed from Barry. It left for the Keighley & Worth Valley Railway in May 1972 and returned to steam there three years later. After years of service on the railway and a second overhaul, the loco is now on display in the Oxenhope Exhibition Shed.

June 1972, BR Standard Caprotti 5 4-6-0 No. 73129

Caprotti 5 No. 73129 left Barry by rail in December 1973, having been purchased for preservation by Derby Corporation. It was towed in convoy with three other locos destined for the Severn Valley Railway and then continued on to Derby alone. Restoration proved to be a long process at the Midland Railway Centre and was completed in 2004.

September 1970, GWR 2-6-2T No. 5572

No. 5572 was removed from Barry in August 1971 after a nine-year stay there. Its first restoration site was situated close to Taunton railway station but restoration was completed at the Great Western Society headquarters at Didcot in 1977.

March 1973, SR MN 4-6-2 No. 35005

No. 35005 *Canadian Pacific* is about to leave the yard. It was destined for Steamtown, Carnforth, with restoration proceeding very slowly. In 1989 it was sold privately and moved to the Great Central Railway. Restoration to working order was completed the following year. After changing ownership several times and years of service on the national network, No. 35005 is now undergoing an overhaul once again.

3 August 1973, GWR 2-8-0 No. 2861

No. 2861 heads a line of ex-GWR locos in the top yard. This loco was to remain unsold in 1990 when Dia Woodham retired and the yard was closed. It was one of ten locos taken under the care of the Vale of Glamorgan Council. Eventually it was bought by the Great Western Society as a source of parts for their 47XX new-build project and the frames were cut up in 2014.

May 1972, LMS Jubilee 4-6-0 No. 45690

No. 45690 *Leander* being prepared to depart Barry in May 1972. After a six-month overhaul at British Railway's Derby Works it began a new career on the national network, being based first at Dinting and later at Steamtown, Carnforth.

3 August 1973, BR Standard 2MT 2-6-0 No. 78059

No. 78059 had been pushed so far along the siding that its pony wheels were completely off the rails. It was to remain there for another ten years before removal to the Bluebell Railway.

3 August 1973, LMS 4F 0-6-0 No. 44123

No. 44123 departed the yard in December 1981 for restoration at the Mid-Hants Railway. It moved to the Avon Valley Railway in 1986, where restoration continues.

3 August 1973, GWR 2-8-0 No. 2861

No. 2861 was to become one of the ten locomotives left unsold when Dia Woodham retired in 1990. It was stored with the other locos under the care of the Vale of Glamorgan Council and was then disassembled in 2014, with parts set aside for the construction of a GWR Class 47xx 2-8-0. The frames of No. 2861 were then scrapped.

3 August 1973, BR Standard 2-10-0 9F No. 92240

No. 92240 became the first 9F to be rescued from Barry when it was moved to the Bluebell Railway in October 1978. Restoration to working order was completed in 1990 and in 2002 it was stored pending another overhaul.

3 August 1973, GWR Castle 4-6-0 No. 5043

No. 5043 *Earl of Mount Edgcumbe* was purchased in 1973 by 7029 Clun Castle Limited as a source of spares for their loco and was transported to Tyseley. In 1997 the Birmingham Railway Museum Trust decided to restore the locomotive and this was achieved in 2008 when it was steamed for the first time. It has become a regular performer on the main line.

17 August 1974, LMS 2MT 2-6-2T No. 41313

No. 41313 was bought for restoration at the Quainton Road Railway Centre and was moved there in July 1975. In 2015 the loco was transported to the East Somerset Railway for a full overhaul before its return to the Isle of Wight Railway, where it will be based.

March 1974, LMS Black 5 4-6-0 No. 45379

No. 45379 left Barry in 1974 for preservation at the Avon Valley Railway, Bitton. In 1996 it moved to the Great Central Railway at Ruddington but was later purchased by the Mid-Hants Railway in 2002 and steamed for the first time in preservation in 2010.

17 August 1974, BR Standard 2MT 2-6-0 No. 78022

No. 78022 had lots of messages of impending preservation, but it was not to be on the Cambrian Coast Railway as the writing would suggest. Instead, it went north to the Keighley & Worth Valley Railway in 1975 and was returned to working order in 1993. It has recently begun another overhaul to return it to the operating fleet.

17 August 1974, GWR 2-6-2T No. 4561

No. 4561 arrived at Barry in 1962. It was bought by the West Somerset Railway in 1975 and steamed there after a lengthy overhaul in 1989. The loco worked for eight years before being stored, pending a major overhaul, which is now underway.

17 August 1974, BR Standard 5MT 4-6-0 No. 73156

No. 73156 was transported from Barry in 1985 to the East Lancashire Railway, where restoration began. In 2002 the loco was moved to the Great Central Railway and is now in the final stages of restoration to working order.

17 August 1974, LMS 4F 0-6-0 No. 44123

No. 44123 was purchased by the London Midland Society and left Barry in 1981 for the Mid-Hants Railway. In 1986 the group relocated to the Avon Valley Railway, where restoration to working order continues.

17 August 1974, WR 2-6-0 No. 7325

No. 7325 was purchased in 1975 and was restored to working order on the Severn Valley Railway in 1992. After years in regular service, it is has now become a museum exhibit.

SR West Country 4-6-2 No. 34105 *Swanage* left the yard in 1978 and was restored to working order on the Mid-Hants Railway, where it has been a regular performer.

17 August 1974

Smokeboxes from every region except the Eastern, with the BR 9F 2-10-0 in the background, including LMS 8F 2-8-0 No. 48151, SR Battle of Britain No. 34081 and a GWR 2-8-0.

17 August 1974, GWR 2-6-2T No. 4156

No. 4156 was one loco that did not make it out of the Barry yard, being cut up there in July 1980 as the supply of obsolete railway wagons for cutting up had temporarily slowed.

17 August 1974, SR MN 4-6-2 No. 35018

No. 35018 *British India Line* went to the Mid-Hants Railway, where restoration seemed to going well but then stopped. It then remained stored until removed to South Coast Steam Ltd, Portland, Dorset, in 2003. It has now been restored to working order by West Coast Railways at Carnforth.

17 August 1974

A view of the main yard with GWR Hall 4-6-0 No. 6984 and LMS 2-8-0 8F No. 48624 nearest to the camera.

17 August 1974, GWR Hall 4-6-0 No. 6960

GWR Hall 4-6-0 No. 6960 *Witherslack Hall* left Barry in 1975. It was returned to working order at the Great Central Railway in 1986 and worked until 2001. It was returned to steam again in 2015 after another overhaul.

17 August 1974, GWR 0-6-2T No. 6619

No. 6619 was rescued from Barry privately and left the yard later in 1974. It was restored to full working order in 1984 at the North Yorkshire Moors Railway and it worked there regularly until its sale to the Kent & East Sussex Railway in 2012.

17 August 1974, GWR Hall 4-6-0 No. 7927

No. 7927 *Willington Hall* looks smart but preservation eluded it. The tender went to another loco and No. 7927, after a long period in storage, eventually moved to the Llangollen Railway to donate lots of its parts to new-build No. 6880 *Betton Grange*.

17 August 1974, LMS Crab 2-6-0 No. 42859

No. 42859 was purchased privately in 1986 and moved to Hull Dairycoates, where it was dismantled for restoration. With the closure of this facility, the loco was moved to a site in Lincolnshire still in a dismantled state. Information about the loco or its future is unclear; the parts have been moved again and the boiler has been scrapped.

17 August 1974, LMS Jinty 0-6-0T No. 47279

No. 47279 was moved to the Keighley & Worth Valley Railway in 1979 and was returned to working order in 1988. Since then it has been a very regular performer on the line and last received a heavy overhaul in 2001.

17 August 1974, GWR 2-8-0T No. 4253

No. 4253 left Barry in 1987 for the Pontypool & Blaenavon Railway, where it was stored awaiting restoration. In 2011 it was purchased by a group based at the Kent & East Sussex Railway and moved there for restoration.

17 August 1974, SR WC 4-6-2 No. 34067

No. 34067 *Tangmere* left Barry in early 1981 for the Mid-Hants Railway. Restoration work eventually began in 1995 and the following year the loco moved to the East Lancashire Railway, where it was steamed for the first time in 2003. Since then it has been a regular performer on the national network.

17 August 1974, GWR Hall 4-6-0 No. 4920

No. 4920 *Dumbleton Hall* is the oldest surviving Hall Class loco and was purchased for preservation by Dumbleton Hall Locomotive Ltd. After being transported to the South Devon Railway, it was restored to working order in 1988. It has been stored out of use since 1999.

2 August 1975, LMS 8F 2-8-0 No. 48518

8F No. 48518 was one of only two Doncaster-built locomotives to reach Barry. Although reserved by various organisations No. 48518 was left unwanted by the preservation movement and became part of the Barry Ten, which were taken under the care of the Vale of Glamorgan Council when the scrapyard closed. In 2008 it was moved to the Llangollen Railway and dismantled for spare parts retrieval. The boiler was required for the new-build GWR County project, the pony wheels for the LMS Patriot project and the cylinders and driving wheels were removed for use on other locomotives. The frames still remain at Bury, Lancashire.

2 August 1975, BR Standard 5MT 4-6-0 No. 73156

No. 73156 had moved from its previous location in the yard but had another eleven years to wait before its move to the East Lancashire Railway for restoration. In 2002 the loco was relocated to the Great Central Railway for the completion of the work to restore it to full working order.

2 August 1975, SR Maunsell S15 4-6-0 No. 30847

No. 30847 was eventually purchased by the Maunsell Locomotive Society and moved to the Bluebell Railway in October 1978 for restoration to working order, which was completed in 1993. It is currently undergoing overhaul, having last worked in 1998. No. 30847, built in 1936, was the last S15 constructed.

28 August 1975, BR North British Type 2 Class 21 No. D6122

No. D6122 had been withdrawn at Inverurie Works in 1967 and was sent to Hither Green for re-railing exercises before being dispatched to Woodham's in June 1968. It was eventually cut up at the yard in 1980.

June 1975, GWR 2-6-2T No. 4115

No. 4115 was one of ten locos taken under the care of the Vale of Glamorgan Council when Woodham's yard closed. Eventually it was bought by the Great Western Society as a source of parts for their 47XX new-build project.

28 August 1975, SR Battle of Britain No. 34070

No. 34070 *Manston* and West Country Class No. 34046 *Braunton* await their fate cab-to-cab in the summer of 1975. Thirty-six years later I photographed the same two locos, both fully restored and in steam next to each other at Washford on the West Somerset Railway.

2 August 1975, BR Standard 2-10-0 9F No. 92212

No. 92212 was purchased for preservation in 1979 and moved to the Great Central Railway for restoration to working order, which was achieved in 1996. The loco has visited several preserved railways since then and is now based on the Mid-Hants Railway.

28 August 1975, GWR Hall 4-6-0 No. 7903

No. 7903 *Foremarke Hall* was transported to the Swindon & Cricklade Railway in 1981, where it was superbly restored to working order in 2003. It is now based at the Gloucestershire & Warwickshire Railway and is a regular performer there. No. 7903 has become the sole survivor of the batch of modified Halls built in BR days.

28 August 1975, SR Maunsell S15 4-6-0 No. 30825

No. 30825's tender shows its Southern Railway identity through the fading paintwork. The loco would lose its boiler in 1980 when it was sold to the Mid-Hants as a replacement for their S15, No. 30506.

28 August 1975, SR Maunsell U 2-6-0 No. 31625

No. 31625 left Barry for the Mid-Hants Railway in 1980. It has been returned to working order and has operated on the main line, as well as becoming No. 5 *James the Red Engine*. It now awaits its next overhaul.

28 August 1975, SR Battle of Britain 4-6-2 No. 34058

No. 34058 *Sir Frederick Pile* left Barry in July 1986 and went to the Avon Valley Railway near Bristol. In July 2011 the loco, which was still not restored, arrived at the Mid-Hants Railway.

28 August 1975, S&DJR 7F 2-8-0 No. 53809

No. 53809 left Barry for restoration at the closed Kirk Smeaton station on the Hull & Barnsley Railway in 1975. After further renovation to working order at Butterley, the loco has worked on the main line and regularly on the North Yorkshire Moors Railway. It is presently based on the West Somerset Railway.

28 August 1975, GWR 2-8-0 No. 3814

GWR 2-8-0 No. 3814 was purchased by an individual and moved to the North Yorkshire Moors Railway in 1986. Since then steady progress has been made in restoring the loco to working order by a small, dedicated group.

28 August 1975, LNER B1 4-6-0 No. 61264

No. 61264 was restored to working order at the Great Central Railway. It worked regularly on the national network before becoming a consistent performer on the North Yorkshire Moors Railway. It has recently returned to service after another overhaul.

28 August 1975, BR Standard 5 4-6-0 No. 73096

BR Standard 5 4-6-0 No. 73096 was purchased privately and moved to the Mid-Hants Railway for restoration to working order. It has been used on many main line duties as well as services on the Mid-Hants.

28 August 1975, BR Standard 9F 2-10-0 No. 92085

BR 9F 2-10-0 No. 92085 was a single-chimneyed 9F which unfortunately eluded preservation and was cut up at Barry in June 1980 when the supply of withdrawn railway wagons had slowed down.

28 August 1975, BR Standard 9F 2-10-0 No. 92207

No. 92207 was bought privately and moved from Barry in October 1980 to the East Lancashire Railway. After much work on the wheels, motion and chassis, the loco was moved in 2005 to the Shillingstone Railway Project in Dorset for the completion of the restoration.

28 August 1975, GWR 2-8-0T No. 4247

GWR 2-8-0T No. 4247 left Barry in April 1985 and was restored to working order on the Cholsey & Wallingford Railway and then the Chinnor & Princes Risborough Railway. It has since worked on several preserved lines before finally finding a home on the Bodmin & Wenford Railway.

28 August 1975, GWR 2-8-0 No. 3845

No. 3845 was the penultimate engine to leave Barry in 1989 for the Swindon & Cricklade Railway. It was then bought by Dinmore Manor Locomotive Ltd and is at a private restoration site at Honeybourne Airfield Industrial Estate.

28 August 1975, LMS Jubilee 4-6-0 No. 45699

No. 45699 *Galatea*, after years of uncertainty about its future, has undergone complete restoration to working order at Carnforth by West Coast Railways and now regularly works on the main line.

2 August 1975, LMS Black 5 4-6-0 No. 45491

No. 45491 was bought and removed by a group of enthusiasts from Barry in 1981. After moving several times it was bought by a private owner and restoration to working order continued at the Midland Railway Centre from 1991. In 2011 the loco moved again, to the Great Central Railway, for the completion of the restoration work.

2 August 1975, SR MN 4-6-2 No. 35022

No.35022 *Holland–America Line* was purchased by the Southern Steam Trust and moved to Swanage in 1986. It was stored pending restoration but was later sold and is now in a dismantled state at a site in Lancashire.

2 August 1975, BR Standard 9F 2-10-0 No. 92134

No. 92134 is the only single-chimneyed 9F to survive into preservation. It has had quite a few homes since being rescued from Barry in 1980. Its first destination was the North Yorkshire Moors Railway, moving to Brightlingsea in Essex before much restoration work to working order was completed at Crewe Heritage Centre. In 2016 the loco moved again to the East Lancashire Railway for the completion of the work.

June 1975, GWR Manor 4-6-0 No. 7828

No. 7828 *Odney Manor* was purchased privately in 1981 and moved to the Gloucester & Warwickshire Railway to be restored to working order in 1987. Since then it has worked on several preserved railways, including the West Somerset Railway, who eventually purchased it in 2004. It has had its name changed from *Odney Manor* to *Norton Manor*.

2 August 1975, BR Standard 4MT 2-6-4T No. 80136

No. 80136 was bought privately and moved to Cheddeton on the Churnet Valley Railway for restoration, where it steamed for the first time in 1998. By 2001 it had moved to the West Somerset Railway until the end of its boiler certificate in 2008. After overhaul at Crewe Heritage Centre and completion at the North Yorkshire Moors Railway, the loco returned to service there in 2016.

June 1975, BR Standard 9F 2-10-0 No. 92214

No. 92214 had been withdrawn by British Railways after a mere six years of service. It then remained in Barry for fourteen years before being moved to the Peak Railway site at Buxton. Restoration to working order was completed at the Midland Railway Centre, Butterley, before working on the East Lancashire Railway. In 2010 it entered service on the North Yorkshire Moors Railway but was eventually sold for service on the Great Central Railway in 2014.

June 1975, GWR 2-8-0 No. 3850

No. 3850 was rescued from Barry in 1984 and moved to the West Somerset Railway for restoration to working order by The Dinmore Manor Fund. It was returned to steam in 2006 and worked regularly on the railway since then. It was withdrawn for a major overhaul at the Gloucester & Warwickshire Railway in 2015.

28 August 1975, LMS Black 5 4-6-0 No. 45293

No. 45293 was purchased in 1986 and moved to North Woolwich. It is now under restoration at the Colne Valley Railway in Essex.

June 1975, GWR 2-6-2T No. 5542

No. 5542 was one of three small 'Prairies' to leave for the West Somerset Railway a few weeks later in September 1975. The one behind was No. 4561 along with No. 5521. In 1979 No. 5542 was sold to a small group of supporters who set about the task of restoration, which was completed in 2001. Since then it has worked on several preserved railways, as well as WSR, and has just received another major overhaul.

June 1975, LMS Black 5 4-6-0 No. 44901

No. 44901 was one of ten locos that had been left unsold when Woodham's yard closed and that were taken under the care of the Vale of Glamorgan Council. In 2013 its boiler was bought by Ian Riley as a spare for his Black Fives and the chassis was moved to Sharpness Engine Shed, the home of the Vale of Berkeley Railway.

28 August 1975, GWR 2-6-2T No. 5526

No. 5526 was moved from Barry in 1985 to the Gloucester & Warwickshire Railway after it had been purchased by a group of enthusiasts. It moved to Swindon Works in 1988, where restoration started on a contract basis. The loco moved again in 1992 to the South Devon Railway and restoration to working order was completed in 2002. It has worked on several preserved railways since then and is now undergoing another major overhaul.

June 1975, LMS Black 5 4-6-0 No. 45163

No. 45163 was transported to Hull Dairycoates in early 1987 for dismantling and restoration. In 1993 the parts of the loco were moved to its present home on the Colne Valley Railway, where renovation to working order continues.

June 1975, GWR 2-6-2T No. 4121

No. 4121 was purchased privately and moved to the Dean Forest Railway in 1981. After some dismantling had taken place it was taken to Tyseley, where it remains in unrestored condition.

2 August 1975, LNER B1 4-6-0 No. 61264

No. 61264 amid piles of scrap metal with the remains of wagon wheels and axles. It was the cutting of wagons that meant the steam locos were left reasonably intact. A shortage of wagons in the summer of 1980 meant that the next locos in line, No. 92085 and No. 4156, were the last to be cut up.

June 1975, BR Standard 4MT 2-6-4T No. 80078

No. 80078 was bought by the Southern Steam Trust and moved to Swanage in September 1976. After a change of ownership it was finally restored to working order in 1999 and has worked regularly on the Swanage Railway. It was sold privately in 2013 and has recently been returned to steam at the Mangapps Railway Museum.

2 August 1975, GWR 0-6-0PT No. 9466

No. 9466 was the only member of the class to survive a stay at Barry, the other eighteen being cut up very quickly. No. 9466 was bought privately and went to Quainton Railway Centre in 1975 for restoration to working order. It first steamed again in 1985 and has since worked on many preserved railways, the main line and on the London Underground network.

2 August 1975, BR Standard 9F 2-10-0 No. 92245

No. 92245 was another one of ten locos that had been left unsold when Woodham's yard closed and taken under the care of the Vale of Glamorgan Council. In 2013 the loco was dismantled, with the boiler moving to another site and the chassis becoming part of a Barry Scrapyard exhibit.

2 August 1975, a View of the Departure Sidings

Part of the Barry Docks complex that was close to road access was used to store locos that were about to leave the yard. In the departure sidings in this photograph were nos D601, 35009, 7200 and 9681. Their fortunes so far have been somewhat mixed; the diesel was scrapped in 1980 and only the GWR 0-6-0PT has been restored to working condition.

June 1975, LMS Black 5 4-6-0 No. 45337

No. 45337 was purchased by a group called 26B Railway Co. Ltd and moved to the East Lancashire Railway in 1984. It was restored to working order there over a ten-year period and has worked on several preserved railways since. It is now based on the Llangollen Railway and has recently returned to steam after another major overhaul.

2 August 1975, GWR 2-8-0 No. 3862

No. 3862 was purchased by a group called the LNWR Preservation Group and moved to the Northampton & Lamport Railway in 1989, where restoration work is progressing.

2 August 1975, SR Maunsell U 2-6-0 No. 31638

No. 31638 had been shunted next to a small BR standard tender for a while. In 1980 it was purchased and moved to the Bluebell Railway. In 2000 it was beautifully restored to working order.

2 August 1975, BR Standard 4MT 2-6-4T No. 80097

No. 80097 was purchased by the Bury Standard 4 Group and moved to the East Lancashire Railway in 1985. Restoration to working order continues at Bury.

28 August 1975, LMS 8F 2-8-0 No. 48151

No. 48151 left Barry in 1975 and moved to the Embsay & Bolton Abbey Railway for restoration and then to a site in Wakefield. It was sold to West Coast Railways and restored to working order in 1987. It has been a regular performer on the national network and is based at Carnforth.

28 August 1975, GWR 2-8-0T No. 4247

No. 4247 left Barry in April 1985 and restoration to working order began on the Cholsey & Wallingford Railway and was completed on the Chinnor & Princes Risborough Railway. Since then it had worked on several preserved lines before finally finding a home on the Bodmin & Wenford Railway.

28 August 1975, GWR 4-6-0s No. 7821 and No. 7802

No. 7821 *Ditcheat Manor* left Barry in 1980 and moved to several sites during its long restoration before finally steaming again on the WSR. It worked for a long time on the GCR before being sold to a WSR-based group. It is currently being overhauled.

No. 7802 *Bradley Manor* was purchased as a source of spares by the Erlestoke Manor Fund and moved to the Severn Valley Railway in 1979. It was, however, restored to working order instead and has worked on the main line and SVR regularly since its restoration.

28 August 1975, GWR 0-6-2T No. 6686

No. 6686 was another one of ten locos that had been left unsold when Woodham's yard closed and it was taken under the care of the Vale of Glamorgan Council. It is to be restored to working order for use on the Barry Tourist Railway.

2 August 1975

A general view of the main yard, photographed from the tender of a locomotive. To the right of the five lines of locos are the sidings for the oil tank wagons and to the left in the distance can be seen piles of scrap wagon axles.

2 August 1975, LMS 0-6-0 4F No. 44422

No. 44422 was purchased by a group of supporters based at the Churnet Valley Railway and was moved there in 1977. It was steamed again for the first time in 1990 and has visited many preserved railways since. It is now based on the West Somerset Railway and is regularly seen at work on the line.

2 August 1975

This is a general view of the yard that was used for cutting up redundant railway wagons. There are fifteen locomotives in this image as well as piles of scrap metal.

2 August 1975, BR Standard 4MT 2-6-4T No. 80098

No. 80098 was purchased and moved from Barry in 1984. It was restored to working order at the Midland Railway Centre in 1998 and has operated on several preserved railways since then.

2 August 1975, GWR 2-8-0 No. 3822

No. 3822 was bought by a group attached to the GWS Didcot. It was moved there in March 1976 and restored to working order by 1985. It has visited several railways since then and has also been overhauled again, returning to steam in 2002.

30 May 1976, SR Maunsell U 2-6-0 No. 31806

No. 31806 looks quite well-matched with the GWR tender shunted next to it. The loco later moved to the Mid-Hants Railway and was restored to working order. It is now nearing the end of another major overhaul after moving to the Swanage Railway.

30 May 1976, SR Urie S15 4-6-0 No. 30499

No. 30499 was bought for the Mid-Hants Railway and removed in 1983. Since then the boiler has been used on No. 30506 and the frames are at Bury for restoration work to be completed.

30 May 1976, GWR 2-8-0T No. 5224

No. 5224 left Barry in 1978 and was restored to working order in 1984. It was later sold to Waterman Railway Heritage Trust and worked on many preserved railways. It is now stored on the Peak Railway, awaiting another overhaul.

30 May 1976

The main yard can be seen in this general view looking from the tender of GWR No. 5952 *Cogan Hall*. In the next line are GWR 2-6-2T Nos 4115, 45163, 45337 and 44901 on the end. The only locos I can recall on the second row are No. 6023 right at the end and No. 3855.

17 July 1976, LNER B1 4-6-0 No. 61264

No. 61264 here is just weeks away from removal from Barry after being purchased by the Thompson B1 Trust. It was restored to working order at the Great Central Railway in 1998 and now works regularly at the North Yorkshire Moors Railway and on the main line.

5 July 1976, SR MN 4-6-2 No. 35018

No. 35018 *British India Line* was photographed two years later than the previous shot (*page 24*). It would be almost forty years before it was acquired for restoration to working order by the West Coast Railway at Carnforth.

5 July 1976, BR Standard 2MT 2-6-0 No. 78018 and No. 78059

No. 78018 and No. 78059 ended up cab-to-cab together at Barry. They are now many miles apart, No. 78018 having been returned to working order at the Great Central Railway and No. 78059 being gradually converted into a 2-6-2T at Sheffield Park.

5 July 1976, SR S15 4-6-0 No. 30499 and No. 30828

No. 30499 and No. 30828 showing comparison of S15 front ends. The nearest one is No. 30499 of Urie design and behind it is No. 30828, a Maunsell loco. No. 30499 remains unrestored while No. 30828 was restored to main line condition at Eastleigh in 1994.

17 July 1976, SR MN 4-6-2 No. 35006

No. 35006 *Peninsular & Oriental S. N. Co.* was removed from Barry in March 1983 by a group of enthusiasts and was restored to working order at the Gloucestershire & Warwickshire Railway in 2016.

17 July 1976

On the departure sidings, LSWR Urie 4-6-0 S15 No. 30506 awaits removal to the Mid-Hants Railway for renovation into working order. This was successfully achieved in 1987 and the loco worked regularly until 2001. It now awaits overhaul. NBL Class 41 No. D601 *Ark Royal* was eventually cut up in 1980.

17 July 1976

This is another general view of the main yard from the tender of one of the locos. Bulleid Pacifics are very much in evidence, with six clearly visible.

17 July 1976, GWR Hall 4-6-0 No. 5967

No. 5967 *Bickmarsh Hall* was very late in departing Barry in 1994, some years after the yard had ceased work. Its first home was the Pontypool & Blaenavon Railway, where it was stored until it was sold and moved to the Northampton & Lamport Railway in 2008. Restoration is now well under way.

17 July 1976, GWR 2-8-2T No. 7200
No. 7200 was later preserved at the Quainton Railway Centre, moving there in 1981, although not as yet restored to working order.

17 July 1976
Locomotives wait for a brighter future in the departure sidings: LMS Crab 2-6-0 No. 42765, GWR 0-6-0PT No. 9681 and LMS 8F 2-8-0 No. 48151. All have been successfully returned to working order.

17 July 1976, SR WC 4-6-2 No. 34101

No. 34101 *Hartland* left Barry in 1978 to a private site near Derby. Further restoration to working order was completed at the Great Central Railway but by 1995 the loco had become a regular on the North Yorkshire Moors Railway, where it is presently undergoing overhaul.

17 July 1976, BR Standard 9F 2-10-0 No. 92219

No. 92219 left Barry in 1984 and first went to Buxton, later moving to Butterley, but remained largely unrestored. In 2014 it was transferred again, this time to the Wensleydale Railway in North Yorkshire.

17 July 1976

In the departure sidings with SR MN 4-6-2 No. 35009 is GWR 0-6-0PT No. 9466. No. 9466 was less than a month away from removal to Quainton Road. It was resold privately in 1977 and restoration to working order was achieved in 1985. It has been a regular performer on many railways since then and always appears immaculate.

SR 4-6-2 No. 35009 *Shaw Savill* may eventually work again as initial restoration began in 2010.

17 July 1976, NBL Class 41 No. D601

No. D601 *Ark Royal* was eventually cut up in 1980 during a lull in redundant wagon deliveries.

17 July 1976, GWR 0-6-0PT No. 3612

No. 3612 was only four months away from leaving the yard for the Severn Valley to be dismantled for spare parts for their other locos. In 1990 the cylinder block and frames were sold to the Llangollen Railway to repair No. 7754.

17 July 1976, BR Standard 9F 2-10-0 No. 92245

No. 92245 was one of the ten locomotives to remain at Barry until it was dismantled in 2013. The boiler was removed to another site and the chassis was stored for a possible future exhibit in a Barry museum.

17 July 1976, LMS 2MT 2-6-0 No. 46428

No. 46428 journeyed to Boat of Garten on the Strathspey Railway, originally as a source of parts for their other two Ivatt 2s, but was then bought for preservation in its own right and moved to the East Lancashire Railway for restoration, which is still in the earliest stages.

17 July 1976, SR BB 4-6-2 No. 34081

No. 34081 *92 Squadron* was rescued from the yard in 1976 and restored to working order at the Nene Valley Railway. It has worked on several preserved railways, most latterly on the North Norfolk. In 2017 it returned to steam after a heavy overhaul.

17 July 1976, GWR 2-8-0T No. 4270

No. 4270 left Barry in 1985 for the Swansea Valley Railway. In 2003 it was resold and moved to Toddington on the Gloucester & Warwickshire Railway, where it was steamed for the first time in 2014.

17 July 1976, GWR Hall 4-6-0 No. 6984

No. 6984 *Owsden Hall* was saved from Barry in 1986, moving first to Bicester and then to the Gloucester & Warwickshire Railway, where restoration proceeded slowly. In 2013 the loco was moved by its owners to the Swindon & Cricklade Railway for the continuation of the work.

17 July 1976, BR Standard 4MT 2-6-4T No. 80150

No. 80150 was one of ten locos that had been left unsold when Woodham's yard closed and taken under the care of the Vale of Glamorgan Council. In 2011 it was exchanged for a turntable from the Mid-Hants Railway, where it now awaits restoration.

17 July 1976, SR WC 4-6-2 No. 34028

No. 34028 *Eddystone* was purchased by the Southern Pacific Rescue Group and moved to Sellindge in 1986. Having completed much restoration work, the loco moved to the Swanage Railway in 1999 for completion, which was achieved in 2003. It has worked on several preserved railways since then as well as being a regular performer on the Swanage Railway.

17 July 1976, SR BB 4-6-2 No. 34073

No. 34073 *249 Squadron* was one of the last four Bulleid Pacifics to remain at Barry. It left in 1988 for the Brighton Works Project and when that scheme failed it moved to the Mid-Hants Railway and is now at Carnforth with West Coast Railways. No noticeable restoration work has been undertaken on the locomotive over the years.

17 July 1976, GWR 0-6-2T No. 6634

No. 6634 was purchased privately and moved to the East Somerset Railway for restoration in 1981. It left the railway in 1999, having been purchased by Waterman Railway Heritage Trust. It is presently in store on the Severn Valley Railway.

17 July 1976, SR MN 4-6-2 No. 35010

No. 35010 *Blue Star* was purchased by the British Enginemen Steam Preservation Society and moved to a bonded warehouse at the Royal Victoria Dock, East London, in 1986. The loco moved again to the Colne Valley Railway in 1996, where restoration continues.

29 July 1976, SR BB 4-6-2 No. 34072

No. 34072 *257 Squadron* was purchased in 1984 and restored to working order in 1990. It worked on several heritage lines, particularly the Swanage Railway, and is now undergoing overhaul back to working order again.

17 July 1976, GWR 0-6-0T No. 9682

No. 9682 was purchased and moved by the Great Western Preservation Group in 1982 to their base in Southall. Restoration was completed at Swindon in 2000 when the loco became the 100th ex-Barry engine to be returned to steam.

17 July 1976, GWR 2-6-2T No. 4110

No. 4110 was purchased by the GWR Preservation Group, based at Southall, and moved in May 1979, the 100th loco to leave Barry. It was transferred to Tyseley but has since been sold to the West Somerset Railway in Minehead and restoration to working order is still a long way off.

17 July 1976, SR BB 4-6-2 No. 34070

No. 34070 *Manston* was rescued in 1983 and restoration took a long time at various sites, including the Great Central Railway, before being completed by the Southern Steam Locomotive Group in 2008. It is now based on the Swanage Railway.

17 July 1976, GWR Manor 4-6-0 No. 7821

No. 7821 *Ditcheat Manor* left Barry in 1980 and moved to several sites during its long restoration before finally steaming again on the West Somerset Railway. It worked for a long time on the Great Central Railway before being sold to a WSR-based group. It is currently being overhauled.

17 July 1976, SR Battle of Britain 4-6-2 No. 34058

No. 34058 *Sir Frederick Pile* was purchased privately in July 1986 and arrived at the Avon Valley Railway. Much restoration was undertaken there but in 2011 it was relocated to the Mid-Hants Railway. The loco became part of the Mid-Hants Railway Preservation Society following a bequest.

30 May 1976, GWR 2-8-0 No. 2873

No. 2873 lost its boiler in the restoration to working order of No. 3803 on the South Devon Railway, where its frames and wheels remain.

17 July 1976, BR Standard 4MT 2-6-4T No. 80151

No. 80151 was purchased by the Anglian Locomotive Group and moved to the Stour Valley Railway in 1975. Restoration work was started there but progressed much more rapidly after the loco had been relocated to the Bluebell Railway in 1998. The first steaming took place in 2001, after which the engine worked regularly on the line. It is now undergoing a thorough overhaul.

30 May 1976, GWR King 4-6-0 No. 6023

No. 6023 *King Edward II* had its rear driving wheels cut through following a derailment in the yard. It was moved to Bristol in late 1984 and restoration began in 1985 but this scheme failed and eventually it arrived at Didcot in 1990, where it was restored to working order in 2011.

20 March 1977, BR Standard 4MT 4-6-0 No. 75079

No. 75079 was at Barry before preservation on the Plym Valley Railway, Plymouth. After some restoration work it was sold to the Mid-Hants Railway in 2007 and moved to Ropley, where it awaits further work.

13 August 1977, GWR 2-8-0 No. 2885

GWR 2-8-0 No. 2885 was looking quite complete and respectable. It was moved from Barry to Southall for preservation by the GWR Preservation Group in 1981 but was eventually cosmetically restored for display at Birmingham Moor Street Station. In 2013 it was sold to a Birmingham-based group and moved to Tyseley for restoration.

20 March 1977, GWR 2-6-2T No. 5193

No. 5193 spent two more years in Barry before being moved in August 1979 to the Steamport Transport Museum in Southport. After some restoration it was sold to the West Somerset Railway and was rebuilt into a 2-6-0 tender engine, No. 9351, and steamed again in 2004.

20 March 1977, BR Standard 4MT 2-6-4T No. 80080

No. 80080 was purchased from Barry in 1980. It was dismantled and restoration work began in the station grounds at Matlock but it was moved to the Midland Railway Centre in 1983 and restored to working order in 1987.

20 March 1977

A general view of the yard photographed from the tender of 8F 2-8-0 No. 48305 with ex-Great Western and Southern Railway locomotives very much in evidence.

20 March 1977, BR Standard 4MT 2-6-4T No. 80072

No. 80072 was purchased privately in 1988 and moved to Swindon Works Heritage Centre, where restoration was commenced. It was later sold to a group based at the Llangollen Railway and was moved there in 1995. It returned to steam in 2009.

20 March 1977, LMS 8F 2-8-0 No. 48173

No. 48173 left Barry in 1988, going first to the Avon Valley Railway at Bitton, where it remained unrestored. It was moved to the Churnet Valley Railway in late 2007, where restoration was started.

13 August 1977, GWR Manor 4-6-0 No. 7802

No. 7802 *Bradley Manor* was purchased as a source of spares by the Erlestoke Manor Fund and moved to the Severn Valley Railway in 1979. However, it was restored to working order instead and has worked on the main line and SVR regularly since its restoration.

20 March 1977, BR Standard 4MT 2-6-4T No. 80100

No. 80100 was purchased and moved to the Bluebell Railway in 1978. It has remained stored in ex-Barry condition since that time.

20 March 1977, SR WC No. 34010

No. 34010 *Sidmouth* left Barry in 1982 after being purchased privately for restoration on the North Yorkshire Moors Railway. In 1997 the loco was sold to Southern Locomotive Limited and moved to their Sellindge base, where the overhaul was started. It continues at the group's Herston Works.

20 March 1977, GWR 2-8-2T No. 7229

No. 7229 was purchased by a group involved with the East Lancashire Railway and moved there in 1984. It was dismantled within days of its arrival but since then progress on its restoration has not been reported.

30 August 1980, GWR Hall 4-6-0 No. 4979

No. 4979 *Wootton Hall* was bought privately in 1978 but was then bought back by Woodham's without it moving. It was eventually rescued in 1986 and moved to Fleetwood Locomotive Centre. It was sold again in 1994 to the Furness Railway Trust, moving first to Lytham Museum and then Appleby station. In 2014 it was transported to their new shed at the Ribble Steam Railway in Preston and restoration work was started.

30 August 1980, LMS 8F 2-8-0 No. 48624

No. 48624 was purchased by a group of enthusiasts in 1981 and moved to the Peak Railway in Buxton. In 2009 it was steamed for the first time after lengthy restoration work, which was carried out mainly in the open. In 2011 the Great Central Railway became its home base.

30 August 1980, SR S15 4-6-0 No. 30830

No. 30830 was purchased by the Maunsell Locomotive Society in 1987 and moved to the Bluebell Railway for restoration at a later date. In 2000 the loco was sold to the Essex Locomotive Society and transported to the North Yorkshire Moors Railway, where it remains in a dismantled state.

30 August 1980, BR Standard 4MT 2-6-4T No. 80104

No. 80104 was rescued from Barry in 1984 by Southern Locomotives Ltd and was stored at Swanage. It was later sold to a group of supporters and moved to Swindon in order to enable restoration. Work on the locomotive continued at Swindon and on the Avon Valley Railway before No. 80104 was returned to working order back under the wing of Southern Locomotives Ltd at Herston. It steamed on several preserved lines, most regularly on the Swanage Railway.

30 August 1980, GWR 2-8-0 No. 2807

No. 2807 was the oldest locomotive to survive at Woodhams and was rescued from there in 1981 by Cotswold Steam Preservation. Restoration began at the Gloucester & Warwickshire Railway and was completed at the Llangollen Railway, where the loco steamed for the first time. It has worked regularly on the Gloucester & Warwickshire Railway and other preserved railways.

30 August 1980, LMS 8F 2-8-0 No. 48305

No. 48305 was purchased privately and moved to Loughborough in November 1985 for restoration to working order. It was steamed again in 1995 and worked on the Great Central Railway before moving to several heritage railways. The GCR became its home base again in 2006 and it has been a regular performer there.

30 August 1980, BR Standard 4MT 2-6-4T No. 80150

No. 80150 stayed at Barry to become part of the 'Barry 10'. In a recent arrangement with the Mid-Hants Railway, it has been exchanged for a turntable.

30 August 1980, BR Standard 4MT 4-6-0 No. 75014

No. 75014 was purchased by a small group of enthusiasts and moved to the North Yorkshire Moors Railway in 1981. Restoration work was completed in 1994 and the loco became a regular performer on the line. For four years it also became the prime motive power on the Jacobite service based at Fort William. In 2002 it was bought by the Dartmouth Steam Railway & River Boat Company and now works on their railway.

30 August 1980, GWR 2-8-0 No. 2874

No. 2874 was purchased in 1987 and moved to the Pontypool & Blaenavon Railway, where it was stored. In 2008 it was purchased by and moved to the West Somerset Railway. It was resold to Dinmore Manor Ltd and they have moved it to the Gloucester & Warwickshire Railway for restoration.

30 August 1980, GWR Hall 4-6-0 No. 5952

No. 5952 *Cogan Hall* was secured for preservation by the Cambrian Railway Trust and moved to Oswestry in 1981. It was sold to Bretton Grange Society in 2010 to use parts from it on their new-build project at the Llangollen Railway.

30 August 1980, BR Standard 4MT 2-6-0 No. 76077

No. 76077 was bought privately and moved to the Gloucester & Warwickshire Railway in 1987. It was dismantled and its parts remain stored, awaiting restoration.

30 August 1980, SR BB 4-6-2 No. 34053

No. 34053 *Sir Keith Park* was purchased privately in 1984 and moved to Hull Dairycoates, where it was dismantled and new parts obtained to help with its restoration. In 1992 the owner died and the loco and parts were sold; however, restoration work was not started by its new owner. In 1997 the loco was sold again and transferred to the West Somerset Railway as a parts donor for No. 34046 *Braunton*. In 2000 the remains of No. 34053 were bought by Southern Locomotives Ltd and over a twelve-year period they restored the loco to working condition. It has been a regular performer on the Severn Valley Railway.

30 August 1980, SR MN 4-6-2 No. 35025

No. 35025 *Brocklebank Line* was rescued from Barry by a small group who later became the No. 35025 Brocklebank Line Association. They moved the loco to the Great Central Railway in 1986. In 2005 the locomotive and the group moved to a private site in Sellindge, where restoration work appears to have stalled.

30 August 1980, GWR 2-6-2T No. 5538

No. 5538 was donated to the town of Barry by Dia Woodham in 1987. It was cosmetically restored at Carnforth and displayed on the sea front at Barry Island. This arrangement lasted a few years but the display was later dismantled and in 2007 the loco went to the Dean Forest Railway for eventual restoration to working order.

30 August 1980, SR MN 4-6-2 No. 35011

No. 35011 *General Steam Navigation* was rescued from the yard for the Brighton Works Project in 1988. This endeavour failed and the loco was moved to Sellindge. A group are now hoping to restore the engine to its original, un-rebuilt condition.

30 August 1980, BR Standard 4MT 2-6-0 No. 76084

No. 76084 became the 143rd loco to be saved from Barry in 1983. Its first preservation site was on the drive of a private house in South Leverton near Retford. After the death of its owner the loco was sold to the Locomotive Owners Co. Ltd and moved to Morpeth for complete restoration, which was completed in 2013. The loco has worked on the main line and several preserved railways including the North Norfolk Railway.

30 August 1980, GWR 2-8-0T No. 5227

No. 5227 was one of ten locos that had been left unsold when Woodham's yard closed and was taken under the care of the Vale of Glamorgan Council. In 2013 it moved to the Great Western Society at Didcot for some parts to be removed for use on the new-build 47xx loco.

30 August 1980, GWR 2-8-0 No. 3855

No. 3855 was bought privately and moved to Pontypool & Blaenavon Railway in 1987. It was stored there until sold and was moved to the East Lancashire Railway in 2010. It is now under restoration, thirty years after leaving Barry.

30 August 1980, GWR Hall 4-6-0 No. 7903

No. 7903 *Foremarke Hall* was purchased by a group of enthusiasts and moved to the Swindon & Cricklade Railway in 1981, where it was restored to working order and steamed for the first time in 2003. It now works regularly on the Gloucester & Warwickshire Railway.

30 August 1980, LMS Jinty 0-6-0T No. 47406

No. 47406 was rescued in 1983 by a group called the Rowsley Locomotive Trust, based on the Peak Railway at Buxton. In 1989 it was sold privately and moved to the Great Central Railway and was gradually restored to working order in 2010. It has worked regularly on the GCR since then.

30 August 1980, GWR 0-6-0PT No. 9629

No. 9629 was purchased by Holiday Inn for display outside their new hotel in Cardiff. It left Barry in 1981 for cosmetic restoration at Carnforth and was displayed in Cardiff from 1986. The Marriott group obtained Holiday Inn and they donated the loco to the Pontypool & Blaenavon Railway in 1995. A group have been involved with its restoration since then, including obtaining its boiler, which had been sold to another group.

30 August 1980, GWR 2-6-2T No. 5553

No. 5553 was probably the last locomotive to leave Woodham's yard at Barry in 1990, having being purchased privately and moved to a site in Birmingham to be restored. It is now owned by the Waterman Railway Heritage Trust and was based at the West Somerset Railway but it is now at the Peak Railway Rowsley site awaiting an overhaul.

30 August 1980, SR WC 4-6-2 No. 34007

No. 34007 *Wadebridge* was bought by the Plym Valley Railway and moved to their site near Plymouth in 1981. It was later sold to a group who became Wadebridge (34007) Locomotive Ltd and moved to Bodmin. It was returned to steam in 2006 on the Bodmin & Wenford Railway and has worked on many heritage railways since that date.

30 August 1980, GWR 2-8-0 No. 2859

No. 2859 was purchased by the GWR Loco Group based at the Llangollen Railway in 1987. After moving to Llangollen the engine was cosmetically restored until the group had completed work on their other loco, No. 5532. No. 2859 is now up for sale.

30 August 1980, GWR Hall 4-6-0 No. 4936

No. 4936 *Kinlet Hall* was secured for preservation by a small group of enthusiasts and moved to Matlock on the Peak Railway for restoration to begin. In 2000, after the loco had been relocated several times, it was finally steamed for the first time at Tyseley. It has worked on the main line and various heritage railways and is now a resident at the West Somerset Railway.

30 August 1980, SR MN 4-6-2 No. 35027

No. 35027 *Port Line* was purchased in 1982 by a group who later became Southern Steam Locomotives Ltd. The loco was restored to working order at various locations and steamed for the first time in 1988. It worked on the Bluebell Railway and the Swanage Railway before being withdrawn with firebox problems. It was sold in 2004 and moved to Southall and then to Lancashire for restoration work, using donor parts from No. 35022.

8 August 1982, GWR 2-8-0 No. 3803

No. 3803 was rescued from Barry in 1982 and moved to Buckfastleigh for restoration by the South Devon Railway Trust. It was returned to steam in 2005 and has since worked on several heritage railways.

8 August 1982, SR S15 4-6-0 No. 30825

No. 30825 has lost its boiler, which was sold and removed by the Urie Preservation Trust for their loco, No. 30499, in 1980. The remains of the locomotive were purchased by the Essex Locomotive Society in 1986. During the overhaul of S15 No. 30841 in 1994, the frames were exchanged and the restored loco became No. 30825. It has been a regular performer on the North Yorkshire Railway since this overhaul.

8 August 1982, SR MN 4-6-2 No. 35006

No. 35006 *Peninsular & Oriental S. N. Co.* was purchased from Barry in 1983 by the 35006 Locomotive Society and was moved to the Gloucester & Warwickshire Railway for restoration. The locomotive finally returned to steam in 2015, some fifty years after being withdrawn by British Railways.

July 1984

The end of the line for the yard that once hosted 297 steam locomotives and now has a solitary resident GWR 2-8-0. Dia Woodham sold 213 steam locomotives to the expanding preservation movement.